C000022639

The Life
I Live
Now

Bea Lauren Reid

Copyright © 2023 Bea Lauren Reid
United Kingdom

First published in the UK by Amazon KDP in 2023

ISBN: 9798375289441

All rights reserved. This book or any portion thereof may not reproduced or resold or used in any manner without written permission from the author, except for brief quotations embodied in critical reviews or for other non-commercial uses permitted by copyright law.

Front cover designed by Bea Lauren Reid via Canva.com

Please contact the author for any further enquiries
Instagram - @wordsbybea

Illustrations from Canva.com

Contents

For the child you once were,
and the person you are becoming.

On Existing

this morning I wake and the sun
is all golden on the carpet.

the half empty mugs and the
twice worn jeans
are evidence that I am alive,
so are the half burned candles
and the dog-eared books
and the way the sky
makes me think of love and freedom.

do the trees know that they are living?
do their branches stretch upward in joy?
do the sparrows and the stones
thank God for their place in the world?
I like to think so.

so surely,
all things considered,
this world is all kinds beautiful
and here I am, existing in it.

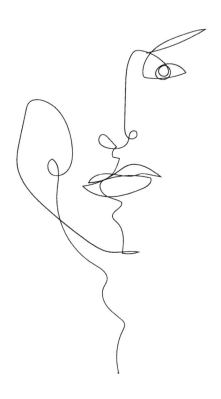

Tea

several times a day i make tea.
and sit in the window,
or the office, or the car.
or stand in the kitchen,
in the bedroom, in the garden.
and for a moment.
all wrapped up in dreams,
i am still.
hands cupped,
thoughts just like curling steam.

Ode To The Rain

how sad it is
that so many people hate the rain.

they run from it's downpour,
speak of nothing but its
supposed dreariness, its
coldness,
greyness.

do they forget its beauty?
the way it dances and
paints the pavements?

do they forget the way the trees
will drink with thankfulness?
the way the rivers will
welcome back their friends
who had become the sky?

do they forget that surely,
if God made the world to be loved,
then loved it should
surely be?

Worried

i am told time and time again
not to worry about tomorrow
but it sometimes clings
to my bones anyway.

sure,
tomorrow might worry for itself
but what if tomorrow forgets
all of the things it promised from today?
what if my hands forget their creator?
what if i forget what it means
to wear the body i have been given
with joy?

but of course,

the mountains do not need to remind themselves
to be mountains,
and the sea does not need to remember,
how to be the sea.
and you do not need to remind yourself
to be loved,
because that is what
you already are.

A New Thing

once, I was brand new.
pink-fleshed and screaming,
gulping in the world for
the very first time,
ready to grow, to learn,
to stumble fowards with
whole heart and wonder.

maybe new years are a little
like that too,
the bleeding of light into
a january sky
just like…
the beginning of a breath,
childlike fistfuls full of firsts,
a running leap into hopefulness.

maybe the earth knows this too.
this wild place!
maybe december ambles out,
and the forests sing
of their soon-to-come bloom.

maybe that's what hope is too,
newness.
courage.
becoming like children
and drinking in life
like cupfuls of joy.

This Body Is A Song

it's living, you see. all of it.
the sharp intake of breath,
the unfolding of hands,
an utterance of love.

later, i remember that i can go barefoot
onto the grass and dance,
or sing.
so i laugh until my lungs are worn with joy.

i think that this is what bodies were made for.
to be loved in this way.
a life-breathed portrait
of bone and poetry and
all the things
that remind me i am living.

i drink tea.
i go to bed.
my body rests.

this life, these shoulders,
are for a small time only.
and oh my!
how glorious and rare
it is to journey on through it.

A Thought Whilst Folding Laundry

i fold up my worries and hang them up to dry.
let them flow in the wind,
skim the daisies with their edges
and part like wings,
tugging and dancing all ghostlike.
i watch -
and for a moment i think this is like prayer,
in many ways.
chaos, stillness.
hoping for a breeze to come
and carry them quickly away.

Common Miracles

i crack an egg into a bowl and out falls
two yolks and no shell.

on wednesday i watch a bird
balance on a clothes peg and sing
into the apricot evening

you twist a cherry stem with your tongue
and spit out the stones

i close my eyes and think of him,
sometimes i think he could have loved me.

there are at least seven
reasons to smile today

there is sunshine on the kitchen tiles

a church bell rings,
and morning comes again

How Wonderful

how wonderful it is!

to wake in the morning and drink coffee
and watch the birds in the garden and
read thick novels
and sing in the shower
and go down to the sea
and breathe in the salted air

and look forward, maybe,
to the sweetness of tomorrow

Hope

I thought I'd grown weary of the world,
with all of its troubles and strife.
I swore I'd grown tired of hope, and hoping.
And praying for some other life.

For what use is hope, or hoping,
When hope never seems to stay?
Until I went out into the dawn
And learned what hope meant again.

Bent down amongst the hedgerows
Amid all the pondskaters, beneath the sky
When you really stop and breathe it all in,
At last, you will understand why.

Praying

It's not always
palms together,
kneeling forwards,
eyes closed.

though it has its time and place.

Sometimes it's the sky - first thing,
hungry for the day
sometimes it's hot coffee or fresh strawberries,
or cold rain.
Sometimes it's loudness, it's angry.
Sometimes it's stillness, it's sticky.
Sometimes it's an open field or a closed door.
sometimes it's a song, a single word.
Sometimes it's grieving, or
sometimes it's gladness but
always - it's a moment of sorts.
a conversation, heart open
daring and hopeful and broken
all at once.

The Forest

this morning i go down to the forest
and wait a while
beneath the branch speckled blue.
silence -

i do not suppose
time stops anywhere, really.
but with peacefulness like this
i do not think it is very much different.

maybe if i wait long enough,
this is what life will be -
stillness, the sky, pondskaters.

but there is more than one
type of living.

soon i will be back in the city,
and that is living too.
that concrete buzz,
trains, and lateness
(time is more real there)

just last week i sat in a coffee shop
and marvelled at how wonderful
people can be.

time, or no time
i think living happens anyway.

even the trees
and the trains
know that.

All I Want

I want to take a moment to breathe. To split the day in two in my hands. I want to know the days ahead and the feeling of freedom. I want to pop tomatoes in my mouth hot from the sun and like the taste.

I want to forget, for a while about the lists, and the dishes, and the creaking spine of the breaking world. I want to stop and point at the lemon trees, and remark "look, lemons!" and remember the taste of yellow deserts. I want to sing.

So loud that our voices break. I want to read old books and watch bad films. I want to be, and I want to was. I want belly laughs and baring hearts. I want real. I want to fall in love like they do in novels. I want newness.

I want home. I want happy and I want whole. I want to be sure, I want to not let it all slip through my fingers again.

All I want, I suppose, is some little place, in this small world.

I've Never Been In Love, But

i have never been in love, but if it is anything like the poets say...

we are in the garden many augusts from now - the hedgerows thick with strawberries - our hair silvered with - the sun and sixty summers on our backs - lips sweet from the plums you swore would never grow - and the crinkles at our eyes are metaphors for joy -

soon we will find ourselves below the caramel moon - and marvel at the stars - how similar we are to them - how small but wonderful they seem! and

we forget for a moment -about the piles of newspapers - on the coffee table - and the unwashed mugs - and the world beyond the garden -

we are sorry! - we will tell the neighbours- we were so happy that we forgot, for just a second- that the world was made of anything else.

How To Wake Up

wake up in the morning and put too much sugar in your coffee. open all the windows and put on the same jeans as yesterday. sing, loudly. burn your toast and arrange your bookshelves by colour. read books that make you cry. watch films that make you laugh.

bake. walk in the woods. write poetry. knit ugly jumpers. cut your own hair and walk barefoot through the garden. make mistakes. make memories. learn how to define happiness in more than one way.

listen to the same spotify playlist you've had on repeat for a year. forget to wash the dishes. get things wrong. remember that everything is going to be ok.

pray. eat chocolate. fall in love. have a favourite flower. take your joys and take your troubles. and go and living also.

The Unexpected Joy of a Solitary Breakfast

the secrets that only I know!
the morning light on the kitchen tiles.
the wednesday morning birdsong,
the pages of the book in my lap.

perhaps this is what they mean
when they talk about magic -

this uncommon peace, suddenly -
as the kettle clicks and billows

Still

the earth sighs,
as she seems to do too much these days.
i think her shoulders are probably tired,
from that ever growing weight,
from holding up all those woes.

but still, joy waits, i suppose.

there is the orange burst of morning,
always on time.
there is the open sky,
belly-born laughter,
coffee,
kindness.

and still,
there is spring,
there is the quiet strength of hope
there is bravery, flowers
love, newness,

the earth sighs,
but still,
light comes breaking in.

Fruit

I come apart like
two halves of an orange
and I am torn, all flesh and pulp
between my own fingers.

Later, I am nothing
but the sting of citrus on chewed nails
and I wonder if it would have been better
had I been a plum.
Or maybe a nectarine.

But there is no way to un-bruise the fruit.
No way to un-tear the skin.
No way to clothe what has already
been laid bare.

I have become the tangerine feast
of my own troubles,
all split segments on a plate.

And my stomach has been aching ever since.

When The World Feels Like It Is Ending

the sparrows in the tree outside my window
are singing again and by now I know their song off
by heart. Much like the way the great oak twists its
branches in the breeze as if it were dancing and the
way the rising sun drips over the fence like a great
glowing yolk.

It's strange how fast and familiar these pieces of
eden become. Much like grief. Or sadness,
sometimes.

But these I find do not stick around quite as long,
or come quite as often. I'm not sure I'd notice the
sparrows quite so much, if they did. Perhaps the sun
would not be so brilliantly yellow. Perhaps the trees
would cower instead and the world would always be
ending.

But life is a precious and wild thing and it is far
too rare and beautiful to not think of tomorrow and
see hope. To remember the dancing branches. To go
to the forest and sing.

Even when night seeps in, the sky comes alive
with moonlight and reminds these tired bones; that
the world has ended so many times, and begun again
the very next morning.

A Train Ride

past the ink washed sky and
scattered streets
the train rattles on.
past the trees, and the bridges -
the lovers and the longing,
the lamenting and the
laughing.
we watch with
wieldy eyes,
all the little lives go by
as we sway on,
softly home.

Maybe This Is My Heart

the way a flower unfurls
and drinks in the day,
so sure of itself,
of its worth,
it's place between the sky
and the dappled earth.

maybe this is a door
to something new,
maybe this is my heart -
opening,
opening,

One Morning

hope,
like wildflower
breaks from below
stretching towards the sky,
persevering.

I Don't Know A Lot About War

look -

i don't know a lot about life,
or love,
or how to end a war -

but i can tell you about joy,
how it hides in the creases
of giving palms.
how it eddies with the lull
of a whispering prayer.
how it, when you really look -
looks a lot like hope.

i don't know much about life,
or love,
or war,

but i know that somehow,
always,
joy will be there.
singing through
the dwindling dark.

Somewhere In-between

i have never been compared - to a shot of espresso -
or my presence to sunlight - but i have written
poems that break my heart ten times over - i have
counted the freckles on my own arms and - i have
sat alone in coffee shops - i have got lost in stories i
will never live - i have burned the toast and - i have
knitted misshaped jumpers - i have cried and i have
laughed - i have danced in heels long past midnight
and - i have touched heaven with my fingertips - i
have stubbed my toes and - played old pianos and -
lay awake and wondered - when - i have loved and i
have lost - and i will do all these things again -
because i may be somewhere - in between love - but
i am - beautifully broken - and human all the same.

A Separation

evening.
we sway
beneath the moonlight,
shedding the heavy day;
separating.

Maybe...

maybe,

  you wake up tomorrow and drink the best coffee you
have ever made. you eat pancakes for breakfast and
don't feel guilty and then you notice it is raining so you
go and stand barefoot in the garden and sing.
somebody tells you how much happier you look these
days and you notice the scar on your elbow from the
time you tried to make moussaka has faded and you
can name six reasons to walk to work rather than drive.
you realise you have loved yellow since you were six
and maybe you haven't changed so much since then
and

    maybe,

  joy is not a version of yourself ten years from now
where you own matching crockery and do not wake up
alone but instead it is the way the light comes through
the kitchen window in the morning and the way that
when you stop to look, everything is a little more
golden than it seems.

Hillary

I go to write a poem in the notes app on my phone about hills and it autocorrects to Hillary. I wonder who she is, This Hillary? Does she walk in the same hills I sit in now? Does she take sugar in her tea? Milk in her coffee? I'm sure somehow that she has red hair, with a choppy fringe, and ties it up in a ponytail every morning. Perhaps she wears glasses, the kind that are slightly oversized and round and she wears perched on the end of her nose. She's a hiker, no, a biker! (autocorrect again). She wears leather jackets and rides up to the seafront. She sits alone on the sea wall and eats salty chips and watches as the world goes by. Maybe she takes out her phone and goes to write a poem about the sand, only her phone corrects her. *Sandy.* So she writes about her instead.

Life Lessons

when evening comes,

i lay back in the grass and
for a moment i become it.
the earth wraps around my fingertips,
the sky and my skin gather as one
and if I wait long enough,
the river falls in rhythm
with my heart.

i think this is what God meant
when He made creation.
this heavy stillness,
this hopeful quiet,
remembering that above us
stretches upward forever.

this must be the meaning of life,
being here.
the faithfulness of the grass.
the rain. the patient trees.
the morning,
waiting to tell the story
once again.

My Greatest Fear

you ask me what is my greatest fear and i tell you, *spiders.* but really i think it might be getting to the end of my life and realising that i forgot to live at all. that i stopped noticing the trees and the soil and the birds. that i never found out what it was like to imagine myself as the ocean, or realised how beautiful and different every person you ever meet really is. perhaps i am afraid that my life will become nothing but lists, and noise, and deadlines. That every day will melt into the next without very much significance. So next time you ask me what is my greatest fear in life, i will go running out beneath the sky and thank it for the spectacular thing it is just to be here.

I Am Not A Poet

I am not a poet until the sky is any other shade than blue, until morning looks like speckled light on terracotta walls. I am not a poet until i remember the way you used to describe it - like waking up to the flavour of joy. I am not a poet until grief settles. Until my arms weigh the same as my heart, until reminders of you are the same as breathing.

And I am not a poet until it is getting dark. Until lonely is as familiar as the way your hands used to rest on my shoulders. I am not a poet until i run my tongue across my teeth and close my eyes, until i imagine you see it all the way i do.

Again - I am not a poet. Until there is a reason to exhale again.

January

january arrives like a hurricane,

as he has done the last twenty-four times we have
met - he is the kind of cold that sticks to your teeth -
determined to fit like new skin - he makes promises
he will probably not keep - typical - and tells me -
but look how different to all the others i am! - he is
all kinds of golden and - there is something exciting
about the way he carries himself - like he will
change you for the better - but now i know better -
but this time he tells me i am not like i was back
then - and i don't quite know what he means - i think
he is beautiful - but he terrifies me all the same - he
opens his heavy arms - and i run to them anyway

Waiting

at sixteen i thought i had defined the ache in my bones as a longing for something not yet quite conceived. a perpetual hum beneath my skin that promised purpose to bloom some day soon,

but even now my heart is an empty church waiting to be worshipped in. my lungs are a theatre where nobody sings but the birds in the vacant eaves. this is the only way that i can describe how it feels to wait and wait until waiting becomes the same as breathing.

and then,

i feel so young yet so old at the same time. i do not think i have ever truly been in love yet all the times that i might have sit folded in the bottom of a drawer.

the list of good reasons i have to be alive gets longer every day but i am still no clearer on the answer.

perhaps i am trying to catch the wind with my hands.

perhaps i am trying to muster an epiphany from the stars.

perhaps we are not meant to have all the answers at once.

but every morning that breaks makes me wonder even more why God has made the sky so blue and is still waiting, waiting, waiting,

to show me how to bathe in it.

The Life I Live Now

I used to be afraid,
of taking up space,
of daring to be seen,

i suppose i'd not learned
what living was back then.
i didn't know the comfort of flowers
or that the best way to feel alive
is to stand, arms wide
in the most wild of winds
and soak up the euphoric strength
of nature.

i was sleepwalking back then.
but,

the life i live now
is spilling over
with the miraculous thing
it is to be alive.

Daughter

If some day I am gifted with a daughter I hope that she will be shaped by joy. I hope that she remarks how beautiful mountains are and that she loves every inch of her skin. I hope she knows that the strength of a storm also resides within her and she knows that it is a brave and wonderful thing to be kind in this world. I hope she finds awe in the early mornings and she finds a hundred different ways to pray. I hope she is every bit the person she is meant to be. I hope she notices the poetry in rain clouds. I hope that when she is asked what it means to live well, she will reply *to love.*

Moon

I am awake again,
and the moon has become
a giant clock face
across the night.

the stars are awake too.
they skim across
the inky sky,
unaware that time
even exists.

Stones Have Stories

Imagine the stories stones must have. Those wise, sturdy things! They must almost be omniscient, the things they have seen, the places they have found themselves. I wonder if the stones that witnessed the first ever sunrise ever crossed paths with the ones that scatter the riverbank not far from here. I suppose it isn't impossible. I wonder if they hold their secrets inside their sea-smoothed lungs, an eternity of yesterdays behind them, many more ahead. If you go down to the river, and listen closely enough, I'm sure you can hear them whisper, gently, to the trees (they must have stories too!) as they roll on by with the water, ready to witness another spectacular day.

When I Fall In Love

when I fall in love, it will be slowly and suddenly all at the same time. like the way a wave creeps in towards shore and breaks open a moment before you expect it too. like the surprising sweetness of a firm-skinned nectarine. like lightning. waking.
i think i will be caught off guard, jelly-legged, tongue-tied. arriving home, somehow but suddenly the most unlike myself that I have ever been.
it will be, I expect, unlike anything I probably expected. You see, there are countless lives and loves that I have pictured for myself. countless different ways that I might sign a letter or make a cup of tea. But eventually it will come down to this.

An opening heart, an opening hand, the unbridled thrill of being known.

Joy, Suddenly...

my bones ache for a life like this.

where the birds dip across the lake and
the oaks stretch their arms to the october
skies.

where the gilded skirts of autumn leaves
bow to the wind. where the birdsong is a prayer. where
the sugar in your tea is poetry. where i am all the
versions of myself at once.

for days like these, a crowded house. of books
and music and laughing. of jumpers and ginger cake
and christmasses. of stories -

of the salt swept coast. the sleety sunshine. the cold-
cracked mornings. of sundays and afternoons and
leather boots.

my bones ache for a life like this.
for somethings and nothings,

the suddenness of joy,
of soaring…

Dragonflies

if you go down to the pond,
you can watch the dragonflies,
stretching out their silver wings
for the first time,
drinking in the brand new air,
twisting airborne
in their emerald bodies
as with their feet
they skim the water
that was once their home.

i think that this is like freedom,
in more ways than one.
the breaking of water,
the thrill of newness,
waking up and learning
suddenly
how to fly.

Brave

i don't always know how to be brave,
or have the right words to say,
or know whether to smile or cry.

but peace, it seems, always finds me.
like fresh rain on the leaves of the beech trees
or the apricot light through storm cloud.

its as if i can call upon it,
grasp it with my hands and
drink it up like hot tea,
waiting for the warmth,
slowly
to reach my aching bones.

Dandelion

I am not a dandelion,
I am a mighty tree.
And I am firmly rooted deep
in who I'm meant to be.

Home

this is home -
being loved in such a way.
this wrapping of arms around a soul,
this promise, eternal.
the Father's heart,
the endless joy
of being known.

Acknowledgements

Once again, the first person I want to thank is you! If you are holding this book, it means so much to me that you have picked it up to read it. Thank You to all my friends and family who have always encouraged and supported me in my love of writing. Every single encouragement, instagram like, comment and book purchase means the absolute world to me. Thank You to my teachers as I grew up who recognised an affinity for writing within me, and helped me to grow in it. Thank You to all of you fellow poets who I have connected with through instagram over the last few years. Its a wonderful thing to have a community of poets who are so encouraging and kind! Finally, thank you to God, for giving me this love for writing. I am so blessed to be able to interact with the world in this way.

Writing, in any form, is a vulnerable thing, and sharing poetry sometimes feels like laying your soul out on a table for everyone to see! If you ever have the desire to write, do it! Be brave enough to explore through words. You might be surprised by what you learn about yourself.

About The Author

Bea Lauren Reid is a twenty-three year old writer originally from Essex. She began writing poems and stories from the age of six, and has loved it ever since. This is her third self-published collection of poetry. She was a runner up in the 2016 Stratford Literary Festival Creative Writing Competition and has also had her work featured in a number of anthologies, magazines, and podcasts.

Bea currently resides in Kent, where she works as a Children's, Youth, and Families Pastor. She also enjoys reading, painting, baking, drinking coffee and being with friends.

Bea also hopes to publish fiction books in the future, with a literary-fantasy novel currently in the works.

To read more of Bea's work, you can visit her Instagram page, @wordsbybea.

You are loved.
You are important.
Your story is worth being told.

Philippians 4:6-7